The Last Day. ctrol

The Last Days of Petrol

Bridget Khursheed

Shearsman Books

First published in the United Kingdom in 2022 by
Shearsman Books Ltd
PO Box 4239
Swindon
SN3 9FN

Shearsman Books Ltd Registered Office
30–31 St. James Place, Mangotsfield, Bristol BS16 9JB
(this address not for correspondence)

www.shearsman.com

ISBN 978-1-84861-793-3

ACKNOWLEDGEMENTS

Some of these poems or versions of them first appeared in *Abridged, T
he Eildon Tree, Gutter, The Rialto, Ink Sweat & Tears, The Interpreter's
House, The Sunday Times, New Writing Scotland, The Cormorant, HU,
Algebra of Owls, Valve, Southlight, Zoomorphic, Butcher's Dog, Poetry
Scotland Open Mouse, Northwords Now, Stravaig, First Time, Pulsar, Fire,
Other Poetry, The Journal, Staple, Scottish Book Trust New Writing Sampler,
Dark Mountain, Cake, Anthropocene, The Blue Nib, Under the Radar*,
and the *StAnza Map of Scotland in Poems*; and some were commended
in the following competitions – Scottish Writers' Centre, Café Writers
Competition and Poems by Postcode/Latitude. 'At the walnut
processing factory' was shortlisted for the Bridport Prize 2020.

CONTENTS

When everything is water / 9

Talking about how blood moves / 10

At the walnut processing factory / 12

Sometimes I can't see out of my car without the windows open / 13

After new year / 14

New media / 15

Birdwatching / 16

A ling time / 17

The hug / 18

Waxwings / 19

Traffic island, A1 near Fort Kinnaird / 21

Helen Duncan's throat / 22

The Clovenfords vineries / 23

November Wednesday AM A68 / 24

Driving in fog / 25

The impossibility of unlocking / 26

Off a raised beech / 27

The lines that twist across paper don't match the road / 28

The shortest day / 29

Standing on top of the National Museum of Scotland / 30

Arctic season / 31

Nesting / 32

The universe as demonstrated by birds / 33

The fish ladder / 34

Teviot in flood / 35

The river in spate / 36

blanket of thistledown over Darnick / 37

The burn bed / 38

A better prospect / 39

Thoughts on an oatcake / 40

Jethart snails / 42

Dragonfly / 43

Hedgehog / 44

Angle / 45

Giant land / 46

City wood above the bypass / 47

Sookin-in-goats / 48

Peak oil / 49

The last days of petrol / 50

The green path / 51

Good intentions / 52

Commute / 53

Idea of my mother / 54

Missing things / 55

Diamond wedding / 56

Bridges seduced by burns / 57

Dave Elder's wheat field / 58

Boundaries / 59

The shopping centre / 60

The taxidermist / 61

Scrogs on a bush / 62

Mustelid research / 63

The walk to school / 64

Breeze / 65

Study of woods / 66

Tree surgeons / 67

No signal at Muchrachd / 68

Blizzard on the hills in spring / 69

Snow on the Eildons like a dusty dog / 70

The garden sea / 71

Uterine dye / 72

The owl pellet / 73

What I see from the car / 74

Song from the edge / 75

French trees by the roundabout / 76

Glass eels / 77

For Faisal and Yousuf

When everything is water

How did we get here? The roads have gone
once there was a network and we plugged into that

buses came for school only to the road end
now they are swept away by the waves.

We are the central point our island of barn and beasts
three children and many thrushes.

There is nothing left to share.
Fodder all squared up.

Once the helicopter came like a bee
drawn by the flowers still blooming by the door.

Talking about how blood moves

Your body is a machine,
it works. Ducts, pipes, tissue, tubes,
the heart belching blood –
a saggy bucket
connecting to three more –
it is impossible to regulate
pressure up and down
and failing
      eventually

into holding pools
      or furred
and weed-clogged canals
to idly loop in the defunct, yes,
industrial complex
and stop.

Your body is not a machine,
the way your heart works
is not architecture and
      not a river system
but this map of tattered colours
embracing all the ports,
the moors, heath, marshes, mountain pass,
      deserts and the sea;
not a road, no, not even
the movement of cars
      ribboning through
            a long high street;

the commute to
necessary extremities.
The smeared space between
wheel or foot or road and destination

is life itself:
the push forward
flux of messages exchanged

a hurriedly made-up parcel
and the desperate race back home.

At the walnut processing factory

The rattle of nuts in the machinery
tings a pitted conveyor belt; piercing

the acrid smell, rich bitter mixed with sweat,
zinging through the bright social distance marks,

factory lights and faded red overalls.
The remaining workers blind taste product

intermittently with languid pick out
and chew and spit; none of the amateur

struggle. Prised kernels are laid bare outwith
a forest more imaginary with each harvest.

A rare memory held in one or two
dry leaves pounded down in the shell discard

echoing beyond the packers' dance steps;
a husk of half-known song on the radio.

Sometimes I can't see out of my car without the windows open

Inside I am listening to Udo Lindenberg
wearing a feather boa in the seventies
drinking kirsch snakebite. There are several
lorries ahead and they all contain animals
or quarried stone; an accident
could reinstate acres of field and dyke.

Outside there's a pink light pressing through twilight
like a bruise, the snappy teeth of pine
all snarled by winds; but I beast the weather,
get the mills generating electricity.
They set to it: all the commuters pay my tithe in bread and sugar
until the salt-licked windows bow down and reveal

that bit of moor again. And it's looking the other way.

After new year

the hedgelines really shouldn't be where they are
it is so easy to change them
look at John Clare one day finding signs and fences

and walls
our neighbour cut a copper beech right down
it took one day

or there are no barriers and the light changes
plants grow in different ways
we have the power

we say we can make this happen
but the first birds at the feeder in the morning
are always the blackbirds and dunnocks

the commuter next door triggers his artificial light
which I reflect back from big and little screens
the windows stop everything
mattering

the line of hand-blown glass

New media

that boy on Soutra in his old car
nothing is the same

at the lay-by where the farmer drops
the feed from his quad bike

the cows in a circle
waiting quiet

even when the hedge brash is burnt
the windfarms grind

except the one forgotten by the wind
he types out requests to other officers

at home, in Edinburgh
he manages the landscape

until the top squall and windbreak
drop off his shoulders

the right man interviewed on radio
lapwings like waves on the plough

Birdwatching

silly fish in the sky almost like starlings
well yes starlings exactly spitting like bacon
or clocks ticking spots knocked and back up

on the toilet they clean the gutter above me
and throw out debris in debt of bugs weevil
anything that takes their eyes

moving in shoals and chattering chattering
imagine them teenagers in the mall
iridescent coats and scarves flying

phones going and noise in all directions
they have sharp claws they are such friends
and then they swim away again

A ling time

Your hair is full of chaff and your head well these little exhalations
remove the straw with blood from executions,
faces of Jesuits, the sunflower flower stalks dry now
heather bells and sphagnum florets,
daffodil cauls close and the flaccid fleshy pig's ear, dock.

All the sad leaves blown up streets and streets of sticky-treed suburbs
ending in your quay-wall contained melt lakes and xenolith moraine

washed out to sea. Our refuse lands on shale, granite, pea shingle
beaches, or sinks undrowned by antler and submerged lea, brash
skeleton boundaries, or exhales probed by oyster-catchers,
pattered by dunlin, sanderling and above
the single erratic skua pierced by a peregrine –

you are the only person to kiss me in the fleshmarket

– the rounded hills, bosomy grass, sheep rocks like clouds,
cotton grass smirred with linn spatter and green shine
birches, mica glint and that sound, that breath of soft wind, shifts
our journey through the black moor on an uncertain path.

Step high, miles to go!

I'll clear your hair, your eyes stay a formal contract of digital crumbs,
field walls, copse, cuckoos like falcons, a clearing – simmer ling – or
this winter ignites paper and the empty boxes
I collect to sail south all while we breathe in the same air.

The hug

god knows if it looks like a hug from the cars on Easter Road
the kind of all engulfing sponge cake hole filling hug from a mother
the kin of warmth and toe tingling kiss of a lover
but it's not; the street is totally empty

when I met you ten foot tall the very shadow of yourself
intent on cuddling the very root of me
tearing its white hidden snail dick self from the tarmac
and rearranging all the fibres in a line with the icy wind of Leith

is that how you make me grow?
is that how you beast me like a bullock with half an ear
and a goofy dangling bawbag one sided too
and the slime of it like cake made from plums

put in a tin warm and phew all foosty
the smell of ten foot of you on a poster in front me
like a poster that has slipped slick with paste
and the dark glasses crisp short pointy shoeness of it

has dropped and fluttered on me to reveal
the whole empty arrow of the road blocked by works
and greggs and estate agents and my feet walking somewhere yes
but yet again crash bang I slip in to the Mash Tun with you.

Waxwings

It doesn't hurt. They've flown away.

The times I don't go down Winston Road:
days flutter past into supermarket, mill, garage.
Below its suicide bridge horizon, Winston Road is a fall thing.

And winter. All the ice from town was dumped
here in the dogging park-up to pock and slide
sodium grit into sticky river past the sewage farm.
Midway the gaswork tank still half-full toads
beside Winston Road, an ancient monument
held up by B & Q stacking shelf meccano scaffolding.

Facing down floral Black Path signposts, bisecting,
once and future railway, shortcuts back the way to town via bushes
and sex attacks. There are pavements both sides
of Winston Road and a 40MPH limit but no pedestrians.
Winston Road is where early I have the best chance
of waxwings, redwings, fieldfare, blackbird, wren, siskin, heron.

I am. All the birds.

In autumn after thrush fall, the speed limit is easy to break
driving slowly; a tankgirl in a soldered hatch
erratic struts of red Ford Ka aching on tarmac.
It is very easy to be overtaken. Birds are hard to see.
At the far end of Winston Road, five cherries grow bigger by the flats,
shed their leaves, bloom depending on the time of year.

Sometimes they are vandalised,
Sometimes not.
Everything drops out of the sky this year in circles.
By the practice pitches, an acre of overgrown dog shit bag hedges

edge the depot, refrigerated lorry park and workshops.
A triangle of access thick with rowan, crap and hedgefruit

empty nature and odd moments;
mostly on Winston Road you are on your own.
But it is all mine without shopping lists, targets or visitors

not even children to be picked up.
A waxing space to grow and throw
every gate, pitch, track, post, black path and bridge open,

wings that could slice the air, be seen
until you fall to earth again
until the beaten roundabout becomes the ambulance back home.

Traffic island, A1 near Fort Kinnaird

It isn't exactly what I expected but then what was that:
blood stains dried beneath the gravel, shards of car and messages
from those who came before sealed perhaps in Victorian glass
bottles, but here in the night with the Forth spread out below
it is at least all mine lit for nothing by carriageway lights.

I briefly consider inhabitation: a hogweed burrow lined with down
sound-proofed or digging underground –
a crab-like coat of containers and wrappers knobbling my home –
or grazing rights, goats perhaps could make a living here
in the flow of salt-spattered traffic.

I wonder if I could or can and pull the dark around me
close and tight; I look at the weeds, and the butts and rags
of hours spent getting past here going to work:
a speck of time marking nothing except interchange roundabout
and for now I know this is exactly what I own; have won.

Helen Duncan's throat

Cheers! Cheesecloth soused as if in wallpaper paste,
ghost body, the cottage by the river led to the silk
shop in X street and sales goods the life of battleships
and witches the men surely drowned whatever your outcome

there's no island like an island close to shore
a step across the channel but the water's deep
a jump across a ditch but you may fall in the current

she transmits and leads she shows the stepping
stones with dainty feet and scones and deep shaded lamps

Helen chewing Churchill into ectoplasm chasms opened
like a dark queen incarcerated although
you always ate well before you showed.

                                                    Easter Road
the long cut between tenements making ha'pennies stretch
until Friday the twisting path between bedding plants
and no step outside is not for you. Hardcore
haberdashery conspiracy theories. Teenager bleacher. Wheesht!

The Clovenfords vineries

All the world purled through glass
and not sure whether this is heaven with
fruit and pools and ferns
or the de'il's place all heat and aisles
sprung with the little spored fronds
that touch and bend

outside the clatter of coal in clarty carts
to keep growth warm from April to dead winter
and the coalman's clunking refracted
and the trainbound grapes packed soft in
Thomson's own mossed crates
bound for London, and the braw shop
in Castle Street; outside
impossible to walk up that hill

put a hand out and it is swallowed
by maidenhair, love apples, Black Alicante swells
next to Muscat of Alexandria and Gros Colman
table grapes eaten with a knife, fork
and a pair of silver scissors, cold lips
plump above the Arabic grate
five miles of hot water pipes
and five boys shovelling anthracite.

November Wednesday AM A68

Soutra cloths and shreds with mist this morning
impossible shiny tarmac and a police van

the Skene lorries chug in front
their own speed limit

not the mist which is illusive
entangling windmills

peer in out of the white still
today the red hedges mark nothing

but the desire to turn the car
rut through the rough into the bracken

and nest up there an opaque hibernation
hidden cut into soft pieces.

Driving in fog

The real thing hugs the car tight:
my little space mummified
in blanket that softens
the road to Edin broch.

I am looking for a needle
in a dream
just to pick up my son
from a small googled house.

But someone has slipped a clear path
through a strainer: the moor fence,
broken and hunted,
all set free to nibble tended crops.

The map serpentines into smaller
ludicrous versions of itself
until foamy, insulated against reason;
a working barn pricks into party light.

The impossibility of unlocking

Tread out on ice and the heart of the water
trembles but something cries out there.
Not the bubble of the curlew
or the moor's last graze of warmth
exhaled as mist
but something animal set in its breath
and the land all aches with the cold,
even the buntings have flown.
There's not a berry on the bush.

Tread out on the ice knowing that I shouldn't.
In the dark walls of loch valley,
the pines glitter and clink with hoar,
the ice heart beats beneath.
I long to get to the bottom of it:
the chasm somewhere deep below,
a quay of warmth opened by your fingers,
but I am intent on rescue.
The ice is something I have to live with.

Off a raised beech

It is a frenzied and chaotic age,
Like a growth of weeds on the site of a demolished building.
    Hugh MacDiarmid

Odd bits of leaves in handfuls in movies chucked out of a bucket probably
I would really like to see you but instead the trees are being precocious
like 70s jeans on teens all patched with colour
or a knapsack of some cool traveller seen on the Metro

buckets of leaves and conker rinds like tangerine peel
gone hard on the stove you cannot really describe this compost as
        palmate, megaphylls,
microphylls, covert bulb scales, thick juicy leaves, cataphylls,
and spines, frondular, bud
stem, the "principal lateral appendage of the stem" including
leaf margin, lamina, petiole,
sometimes dorsiventrally flattened organ, isobilateral, an amount of
epicuticular wax, then kinds of leaf-like structures that appear leaf-like,
        phylloclades and cladodes,
and flattened leaf stems, phyllodes, the phyllids, some foliose lichens

and in amongst all this pixellating nonsense I am chasing after you
stubbing my toes on biscuit tins, the walls, bodies, water tanks and keys
concealed by mounds and mounds of the orange stuff –
mini-killers my grown up sons used to call our leaves
and we had to run fast before they touched us
sometimes straight in front of traffic –

and meanwhile you limp away in black cool but not a traveller very
        stay-at-home
with tiny children and guitars and linguistics
and all that medieval shit
and what has this to do with stones and weeping and Kelvingrove unleaving?
I mean can't you just wait: I was in love with you.

The lines that twist across paper
don't match the road

There's a left turn here into your bedroom
that I know well; yes
I confuse my right and left but this is simple.

Turn left and find an open door:
three weeks to the shortest day
but the bramblings prick thick berries in a hedge
on the unmade road to Synton;
days spent on cropped turf by Blackcastle Hill
repopulating settlements;
planting stubby trees that in turn
grow large, fruit and bear the weight
of migrating birds; bark brushed
by a long-lived beast.

Turn right and the animal is me
caught in the headlights of a West end flat.

The shortest day

The Roman road on top to avoid ambush
up the three mountains past the watch tower
and the ten gated houses

crouching like a lion in the scoop of a dune.
We are down here with the wood at our back
friable as a good loam

the deer penetrate the birds shatter the screen of branches
and leaves fall
revealing the flat frost of a field I cannot place.

There is a loch at the top covered in ice
and a promenade of geese a handful of wheat
gold finches thrown into the wind in the dun blown land.

All the garden is in pots dollops of earth and
a nursery-labelled resistant jungle it inside and out
armfuls of wood-carried holly.

There are three female trees and I have cut them
twisted my banisters into a forest
and no one not even animal can break that cover.

Standing on top of the
National Museum of Scotland

We find the roof garden.
Its little patch of moorland, birches,
heather so perfect it might hide
grouse turd, quartz, even Tunnock wrappers.
A mountain peak handkerchief
picnic-pack pooled
until the air all around is streaked with dry
leaves and the ghost of pollen.

And the sky opens out above all the glass
inaccessible VIP pathways.
How did we get here like this?
And the face of volcanos: did I mention
Arthur's Seat with its buzz cut of tourists?
Will one of them fly?
Fighting vertigo with talk and tin cans,
the children snail the big rocks,
impossible here, and the glinty light
changes. And I feel happy
lifting off slightly over to Blackford Hill
and Salisbury Crags, bigger than
anything this family thing.

And as we trooped down to the café;
the blank plastic clock below
cried out the hour like birdsong
telling me later
that was the moment that you died.

Arctic season

Wolves chew on my electric fence for fun, its pennants,
against a sweep of hill and water and yellowed grass.

This is summer and the blades are thick with birds, hare
and rodents play here, running farther

than necessary, secure in extra calories.

In my tent, I am the broken bell in this landscape.

Five miles away from the small meteorological station
instruments under my care:

the things that, in a university room, I hold dear,
all stretched against a blue sky and tussocks.

My ideas clang against the urgent matter of intake
and activity, sex and childcare while that lasts

followed by the infinite
peeling rags of winter.

Nesting

The scrape of rustled beaks hunting for moss and hair.
The kind that blows out and up.

Swifts use bus tickets and feathers
although they might never come to land
– they have no feet, the monks said,
they fly until they die.

We all of us search for homes in the sky
and keep on going in the face of logic:
key rings with rabbit's feet,
granny's souvenir knives, the old cheese frame
from Wisconsin,

carried in box and plastic bags. We circle our world
ridging the space like curled serpents

but our fragile homes built on aerial dreams
as a matter of fact share nothing.

The universe as demonstrated by birds

The pampas grass is full of sparrows harvesting
last year's seedheads they are the children of the
children of the children since I have been here

trying to control weeds

they vector it and make an astrolabe
demonstrating all the planets, asteroids
and circling orbits

the flutter of their wings like the sound my ears hear
sometimes when waking from the dream
of meadow when I shrink below the grass

an atom – rerum – everything grows out of me
and contains itself and the seedheads chatter
like old friends; perhaps death.

The fish ladder

A toddler's walk to the lake's edge
and its two bridges hugging the shore;
a freshwater beach and low wall
ideal for my son to splash in;
there's nothing wrong here.

Just the bluish cushions of water
piled like a child's game to avoid:
the current's fast; no ladder
but a conveyor belt of lust,
Rapunzel's hair skeining over.

This thing must happen.
Milt and roe on the gravel
and smolt, fragile as ice, sharding
down the river to the sea.
This place not memorable is known:

salmon die for a second sight.
Rucksacked, the baby cries for home.
We climb, all snacks gone,
to a rented cottage and maps.
I don't think I'll get back.

Teviot in flood

Something quite dry and spare
lights these woods; a wind
in the trees and by the coalshed;
in the kitchen the fug
of a scouring sauce pan's steam
and the baby asleep next door.

The river is below behind the back door.
Again and again the staff shows waders topped.
Six feet of flood –
all the fisherman's stakes washed away.
Fields stretched with water: impossible – frothed,
red-brown from the tributary Oxnam,
and chopped with twigs and leaves,
and deep down silver fish.

And through the let cottage window
I examine the mute managed woods.

The river in spate

The heron is up here by the house eating mice.
There are 3 on the field verge. A siege.
Water coats their grey backs and they stand
Uncompromising. The field where the houses must be built
is lapped with water. Drainage changed
and meadow is burn.

For the birds this is the stream edge
where they can feed on what lives in shallow water.
The kingfisher takes it perch on the outside light
to dive for minnows. Oystercatchers shriek and make a home
on the kennel. The water flows.
The house becomes tributary.

blanket of thistledown over Darnick

until you see its movement
a billion long-haired daddies
or something pulled about
by an almost wind
an obsolete stage prop
half secured

white threads that split
like webs jammed
against the hedge they flower
and in the stones of
the dry Huntlyburn
they shiver like minnows
at their last breath

lie down in Bessie Reid field
and I could wear a coat
of down flinching
as I panted out fibres
eyes broken by lines
pixellated goldfinch harvest
how can I remember this?

The burn bed

The stepping stones of the ford
mosaic the mud
unseen
for a generation.

That last pool endured
days of scum and midge
pokes for fry
until it too was dry.

Desert scrolls and stones
litter this new path
beneath meadowsweet walls;
the depth of the pot

attracts a shoal of blackbirds
to hoe its moist furrows.
Alight.
I wake myself to follow.

A better prospect

Think I grew up in channels and steps:
the water that drained from the ornamental lake
and the culvert grinding against quartz stone
at the beginning of each rainy autumn.
I am down here cleaning out the leaves, the stink
of fish left in a rare April sun,
a hound dog's bones, the tears of my lady.

I like the canal and its taut purpose;
its path to industry; it seems to match my mind
or my body for I feel the feet that walk
its tunnels; they beat inside
to be free; and you are always the river
that bounds the estate in laughing curves
and sprays of primrose; that small burn
I took eight years ago, and bent to lordship's pattern.

Thoughts on an oatcake
taken from a dead Highland soldier after Culloden

a biscuit a biscuit crumbled crumbled
and eaten on a battle morning
in a glass case and a ball beside it
the ball a bullet clean now under glass
blood that dripped on grass from
the white skinned chest and an arm
on that green grass the skin white
above the weathered tan and the pattern
of veins small and blue in white skin
on green grass the blades
drip with blood under glass
the ball all clean and the biscuit
from the pouch is clean and crumbled
a little taken to keep the spirits up
and the rest to be saved for later
a wife had said or a mother
and the biscuit that perhaps the crofter
or the boy or the labourer
had with forethought saved
wrapped in a small bit of cloth
or handkerchief for the evening
protected there as he left it
the crofter or the boy or the labourer
laying down in the grass quite softly
apologetically white upper arms
soft and childlike known only to a mother
or a lover revealed and pressing softly
the pattern of thin blue veins
on the green grass and the blood
quite clean drips steadily
as the heart continues its work
for short while and the grass its seeds
or lack of them remind this man

of the harvest and the sun and the sky
emptying above him so still around
for a battlefield the evening gathers
and the biscuit crumbled
ready under glass still waiting
and the ball beside it
stopping the heart's work

Jethart snails

Sweets for funerals: would you like one of the last
from the paper bag he left behind;
each boiled drop wrapped in cellophane,
every day could be a Christmas.

These came in a tin. There's one still
in the back of the cupboard with the grocer's
logo dreamed up by a Frenchman.
Hence the snail or was it the shape?
In the old factory – the back of a shop –
an apparition clung to the walls.
Forget Wonka.
Here is where it all started.
The toffee mentholated hung from a hook
each Monday
and pulled down by a week of gravity
to get the fine texture;
the *escargot* swoop and roll.

And when you left that shop
you were a little candied too,
following the road through the snow
up to the gaol and museum closed today;
ghosts at your shoulder
that you walk through like the flakes
that leave no footprints;
suck and mould with your tongue
until the tin is empty
not even sold here anymore.

Dragonfly

He sits by the gate's latch flat against the red bricks
and watches nothing. The cut-glass eyes have no insight
and my breath, on wings filigreed with black veins
and copper, makes no impression. The bunched muscles
on thorax extend into golden stripes twice bisecting
the wing cage. And his abdomen jointed leads
to two evil spikes: these I am told cannot sting.
Under such close scrutiny, he never stirs or
moves the goggled psychedelic head. And will not face me
but flies as soon as my back is turned: leaving an absent
shadow in the place he'd touched and quietly burnt.

Hedgehog

close not furry not laundress but sharp thorn-ridden
fighting territorially with hisses and crashing foliage
of a large animal in the dark boar-strut
territorial droppings on the end of paths and steps

long-legged climbers and sometime bedraggled mother
during daylight late spring feeding of young
out and hardly shy only absorbing leaf cover
as necessary their paths networking May undergrowth

I know where they go ripping slugs from earth
rent on a damp night crunching snail shells
all teeth and broken claws
my granny's lore was
to reveal the curled ball of them
stroke like a hairbrush on top of the bristles
and they will follow you unpicking maiden locks

Angle

the fleets are out this morning
they sailed through
the harbour of my garden

before dawn
an invasion
fishing rights all their own

each plant is pocketed with net
seed heads carrying great drifts
and skeins of silk

down to the smallest
landing basket in the wet grass
the owners are absent

only drizzle gives each web away
points of light
and prey

Giant land

It was the cat more than anything.
Children amuse themselves by lifting it,
the king said nibbling a hazel pear
but I could hardly lift a paw.
We were all beaten and me three times.
The riddles, yes, the woman was age,
of course she pulled me to the ground
and the horn contained the sea.
I drank ports dry; exposed the marsh land
putting the eel farmers out of business.
Loki battled fire and it consumed all.
And the boy ran against thought.

That last journey home some by boat
searching for the crag and the landscape
all changed by the dropping water.
The fish putrid in the slop of mud exposed
and the walk to the pier head longer
deep steps on inconstant ground
and the expected fire somehow colder.
Today in my hall, the boys mob and whistle
a farm cat braced against their chests.

City wood above the bypass

I am walking through the machine gun wood
looking for siskins

in the wood someone has hung mirrors on every twig
my reflection in raindrops

the path is needled and high above
the pitched notes of crossbills

and goldcrest
are the blown wires that tear up the sky

but I am looking for siskins in the pinewood
and instead I only find me

Sookin-in-goats

sunken path through the wild garlic
we could sell to tourists
health walk the heady stink it is isn't it
the gorge an armpit sweating
out this cooked smell

in its crease far below a pattering stream
still erodes the sandstone
beneath the thorn and scrub
impenetrable goldcrest song
the slightest fly stab movement

a cottage so perfect with its row
of beans and weatherboard wood store
hides from beach wind
we walk right out into the mist
past every kind of known rockpool

until we find Muir's goatsucks
a Norse remnant? put a hand in one
touch its cool depths and you are dragged under
into kelp, stones and gills
only one portal out of nine hundred

on the shore rocks sandpipers
are busy disappearing
into the sea morning fog
so busy until their bodies are cut in two
and pop back together again

the tide is coming in and will
wash up the beach, next the cottage, one day
the garlic, the tourists, the viaduct
where our car is parked, eat up our very home
blow us down it is before we'll see

Peak oil

Around the steading dairy's abraded foundations
the green shadow of dusty hazel uncoppiced
radiating warblers on the edge of the clearing
inside the rig still pumps amongst the ivy its ranch
men posture in a prefab kept right after so many
years their company logos worn smooth on overalls
that they both appear to wear all night all day

while the space gets smaller an owl pocket
now as the long grass around the machinery harder
to manage vole tunnels the kestrel ceiling
the sky that once seemed so big
at night sleepy hands must nurse webbed gauges
blockages in the system more frequent pneumatic
suckle the output at most one pail of rank milk.

The last days of petrol

The ebb of a country lane and meadowsweet;
or those hot verges seen from a corner
for a second brown itching with seed; and
the stop by an unfamiliar signpost;

the humpback bridge over a chub stream
taken fast so the belly flops;
driving up above the mill to get away
from work with a teak chest

wedged in the back of a hire car
until the National Trust car park
reverse in and out again and back
across the moors to keep

away from the hotel; the solitary race
from home to the North
faster each time until the street trees
perspire sap on the bonnet;

chug of petrol in the last border garage;
driving round the block and round the
block and round the block
and round until I am no longer

early; empty journeys
fast except by speed cameras;
and the trip to the shops
things nobody needs packed

by a teenager; the edges of shopping centre
a route for dogwalkers as the last smoke
coughs and stops on the slip road;
the grid flows into green lanes.

The green path

Walk out on the turf above greywacke and siltstone
laid down at the bottom of the sea
500 million years ago. Walk out
into air pocketed with kittiwakes, guillemots, razorbills, shags,
herring gulls, fulmars
who nest in the creased ridges of the folded Head
volcanic lava flow.

The turf cuts between pink tufted chasm
and abyss patterned into gullies
and sea stacks ideal for nesting sea birds.
And for dreamers who take this path
roll the green carpet right out to sea
and its gannet pierced tidal slop
of toothbrushes and tampons and wire and algal bloom
back into Eden again.

Good intentions

Really the lighthouse isn't important compared to the visit to the beach:
its wires, beakers, nets, four footballs, seaweed entwining burger boxes,
    eskies,
film, gauze-like micropore filaments, a dead deer, bunting, oil cans,
    plastic bottles
filled with fizzy drink that still glows red like the sunset behind clear hills,
legless Barbies, the sweatshirt of someone big and absent, carpet, toys
    abraded
into nightmare in the twilight, sheeting and tarpaulin, covering uncertain
mounds, off-cuts with nails that grab at legs in the gathering, and
the only place to camp discounted by a putrid smell.
This is a latrine. We take the small white path that creeps back onto
    the moor.
We vow to remember and clean up the sea.
The headland lighthouse flicks on and off.

Commute

the water on the road
the leaves in beaten hedgerow
the beat-up car leaves
the water on the car
is flicked off by the wipers
there onto burnside road
the brown water in the burn
the hill it scours and turns
water stronger than the rock
the water on the road
never stops culvert hedgerow
beaten back and lochans
stand in fields can't stop
the rain the beaten-up car
bites through on its way
the water leaves and hay
steams in stacks
at ploughed field edge
the tractor chews the herbiage
brown water on the road
the hedge sinks into the dark
the light leaves a beat-up sky
I go this way just to get home
the water on the road

Idea of my mother

a radio ragbag of melody
broadcast a song
or the job I didn't want to get to
or the fast lane slipped past
clipping approaching cars into jolting
squares between crash barriers
or my hands were cold
on the morning steering wheel
or a farm on a hill within its own wall
shone red in the sun
or I wanted to check my wallet
for a ticket or credit card
and couldn't or love had gone
or some fur once animal lay
tattered snapped back at the roadside
or some other bitter magpie
extracted tears large and gainless
as motorway speedtraps for her absence

Missing things

Easy as an egg, the green crust breaks
breathing smoke. A compost vulcanologist,
my hands found heat: its miracle
shared with slow worms.
Like fingers entwined, lithe, silent
and gone when I show you
the shock of empty banana skins and shells.

You never see what becomes
the cock's snack, the cat's target practice
while my sons inch their cycles past
or pull *worms* rigid as a stick
with resistance from the debris
by the outhouse. Sight can't be conjured.
No science manages our intercourse
and by tidying the old iron sheet
the population is lost.

A retreat to the allotments next door
lists terraced composters, undisturbing coughs
and the stoop to weed and hoe.
Occasional boys in the village find out,
are shown how and where.
The flick of the dustbin lid:
the dragons sleep. A second late
a heat held only by being missed.

Diamond wedding

That rain a fine drizzle and your memory
a butterfly sitting it out on the pelmet
who is she? you ask again
who is she?

look at the smirr on the pane
every bit of colour pixellated
a butterfly's wings scaled like snakeskin
don't try to hold it

its weight in flakes dropping
drifting in wet wands on the buddleia
all the colours are mixed up outside
and the big tent what is that

and your daughter one of five
a row of them separated only
by relative size under umbrellas
faces pointed by white

raindrops flowers grass

Bridges seduced by burns

Come with me, forget your fingers of mere
reeds and whitethroats –
whole grass seed peace –
the muir fall of autumn.

Don't you want to see
the tidefast end of it all;
stanchions stabbing the water in
the battle of tide, crusted shell and freshet?

This is your migration.
Why always be the one returned to?
Your aching boards only a recipient
of fox pad and mustelid scrape –

that pontoon pause – come
feel even your structural bricks, all neat and tight,
shuck away like pearled eyes,
stream deep into my gunshot flood.

Dave Elder's wheat field

the space beneath the cushion reed's rush
is where I will burrow
a self hollow the shape of a tunnel
where I snake to examine clouds

a perfect corner of cloud in a rough silk
creamed a blanket sacking coloured
and the ears in my hand almost milky
edged like a cornice

each ear just so
and in the tussled warmth of mouse grass
below I bury my head and keep
out of sight a field's space

Boundaries

walking in a new place is so suitable for the foot
that path with different levels small stones
and moss that is not wet
I don't see any violets
or siskins or goldcrest or anything interesting
but the air smells good
my foot is connected to my legs and hips
and it is stretching out and walking
right round that bermy bend where the marsh
edge gives a little
there really are no police cordons here

The shopping centre

The edges of snow remain pushed in berms around the car park.
Light from the Gala prinks the tarmac right up to the millstream.
I am going to Tesco's. Past the urban bedding and granite,
the line of snow is ridiculous. Everything erased but this
like a child's drawing. A memento of winter not finished
but started. A frame that makes my steps and recyclable bags
stop washed in bright potential, a spring empty of bulbs yet.

The taxidermist

Feathers of duck and debris on the Turkish carpet
the outside of things settle
back to the woman in the forest
glimpsed from the river path

there was no one beside me in the rain
and the woman was all lights
glaring brow her red hair
tressed with cones

there was no one beside me
nor ever likely to be
and this woman was the queen
of sketches behind glass

really the ducks come into it hardly at all
just the down of them
in the damp she left
as lifelike as I could make it.

Scrogs on a bush

Scrogs on a bush
by the river
in the hedge
reeking of fox.

Does fox eat scrogs?
They lie
spang-ed
by the tree.

A burrow through briar
stretches
to the kinnen field;
straight to scrogs.

Or scrogs to coney?
River treacles past
after flood
brown as rotten

scrogs on a bush
by the river
in the hedge
reeking of fox.

Mustelid research

The pile the known pile they always
they always mark on paths and junctions
in grass paths, burns, inlets points of crossing
the pile they always mark the pile

the spraint of how many on a raised point
a law of spraint where how many pass
and pile the mark the smell
down in the nettles with you, thighs burning,

head to the liminal ground and gulping in the
webbed pressure, not dogs but claws
lines the slip down slap to water,
how many the pile marks spraint,

otters passed this way separately or
together, it is all you will confirm,
the smell of the spraint fish and fish
and jasmine tea.

The walk to school

Our path's geometry through the purple-headed grass
is mappable strong lines and blunt angles
a point of divergence when the stream is dry
or if we are in a hurry
an irregular quadrangle coinciding at the entry
to the rugby field

Its four corners marked by
fox's territorial dropping
the nailed-shut gate of Bessie Reid's field
a dead hedgehog
a sign prohibiting canine fouling

Within this structure are the dandelions
whose stems we can only kick free to convert
after the clocks have ticked away
swallows pink bellies just above them
that I always mark as martins
falcon pellets in the dried-up burn bed
or wet all-terrain sandals
and a plank bridge that does not fit the water

It doesn't connect
a balanced spring dislodges
the wren's nest
the kestrel and one fieldfare
pinecones and the worn-out path
the council try to discourage
salvageable litter on Abbotsford Road's pavement

The weather we have learnt always and never perfect
in the scheme the nature of things

Breeze

The breath we take today
rips in from the estuary mudflats.
Nobody gags at its taste
or stink: a supermarket trolley heft
from an old pond's margins;
sewage suck; chrysanthemums
left in a vase of water.

Wind's not important here.

North-easterlies pitch sly
particulates sucked from exhaust.
And veering back reek and sting,
filtering the refinery's plumes.
It's no more of a pain than onions.
All kids get summer colds. Imagine
if we lived in the town.

A south wind vents the comment, "It's balmy."

Study of woods

our research into each other
your palm on the ground cover grid
we mapped next to the white bluebells
and my dog's mercury stomach

the population we note is growing
our results marked in midge bites
that indicate
even after our shift is done

Tree surgeons

Waiting at the red light I watch the men take down the last oak by the
      new builds.
They tidy up its sticks and twigs all summer leafy self-conscious
like girls after a dressing up session,

armfuls of foliage awkward toppling.
Above a man on rope tiptoe shapes his way into the curve of the last branch
lops it delicately in pieces down and drop down

to the waiting handmaids careless of danger with brooms now;
the tarmac must be easy for the filed cars to pass by.
The oak is the shape of an empty clothes hanger as I drive through on green.

No signal at Muchrachd

The Cannich is shrunk into pits and holes:
a mould of itself made by electricity
that the swallows test and chip
for distortion.

Waves of static insects caught in their eyes:
a software map of the valley
everything still
and especially that birch shining on the hill
imitating a phone mast
so real it is fake.

And then all the dot dot dashes are only
swallows and midges and fledgling twites dropping from the gutter:
a delivery of information packages
like a thirties' love story
or Richard Hannay motoring too fast round corners
to save the world – and me too,

an actual eachway trip of 4 miles
to pick up the messages.

Blizzard on the hills in spring

An infinite wire fence on each side nothing but snow
the boundary itself curls like a barbed creeper bent up then down
animals struggling to get to feed

but there are no beasts here
just a path of beaten down footsteps in the lee of the posts
the white on all sides the dogs and mine

this is the only line we can follow on a blank map
everything is flat we fly high up above the dykes
somewhere in a hollow deep beneath sheep breathe still

Snow on the Eildons like a dusty dog

The otter was on the cauld today in the end of the snow hunting for packages in overlooked thaw larders Found the stoat trail again in the snow this morning and it spiralled round and round – maybe dancing, maybe charming a rabbit

Mouse motorways uncovered in Bessie Reid field – snow has melted to show intricate grass bobsleigh run forms sculpted writhing; rodent roadmap. Burn edge thick with little birds: wren (alone, territorial), later goldfinch, chaffinches…all searching for granular fast unfrozen food

Gang of Scandinavian blackbirds have taken over the garden all puffed out against the cold as if on steroids Obliged to wear the long johns of an adolescent boy. Rolled and slid home an armchair scavenged from the dump – at last the snowy weather is good for something

The garden sea

the cold air's met the hot air and now the washing's all flying
is it dry? the wind like the wind at Tarifa, the promontory
and shuddering windsurfers' tents and the African ferry
drawing in drawing out away it goes on the edge
of everything. A journey from the crooked paving stones
some hot some cold in the shadow greened with algae
and a dead snail shell the thrush the agricultural smell
the heat the wind the soft sigh of something beginning
ending the garden the children home from school.

Uterine dye

A picture of lakes, deltas and flood,
water meadows sponge
the bikini womb up delicate meanders
evaporating into the abdominal cavity:

the cannula is draining beyond the uterus,
its deluge of radiographic dye,
fill and spill, fill and spill
as natural as the wash of menstrual tides.

An industrial landscape of canal basins
curbed by careful Victorian bricks,
reveals the control imprint is patent
or blocked. Perhaps by scarring, polyps,

fibroids are debris in a storm drain.
But we can change the weather,
scour the channels like a thunderstorm.
The child in the culvert slips out breathing.

The owl pellet

I put it in my pocket wrapped
in inadequate tissue; it works free
and at home appears lost
until, beneath the debris of lip salve,
paperclips, paper pellets to be discarded
and a shoelace, I catch its essence,
the bladderwort of it.
On the windowsill it tells the weather:

a mermaid's purse on a dry riverbed,
the drop from a familiar perch,
a sinuous gorge on the mud,
and desiccated lichen its intestinal shape
suggesting dropping;
its light weight and durable package
permitted a posting into the pool
no longer pooled.

Much later the unwrapping
because it merged with the crumble
of the stonework becoming
cuttlefish shell and secateurs.
It resists the prod of a stick or skewer
that skin thick and pudding-like
breathing back against imprint;
until thwacked with a trowel

it spills a cargo of fur and ivory;
the claws of huge rodents hunted in field guides
until the goods left to bleach
at the flowerbed's edge descend
from fair price to articulated felt
a graveyard by the seashore;
bodies enveloped in beads and blankets
song all washed away.

What I see from the car

This particular road is unmade
veering between council oversight
and quad bike trail
not quite unadopted but close
sometimes its beech hedges beckon each other
across the washed-out culvert.

A green rime skins its surface
through the plantation; the unused centre
soft with moss and cleavers.
There's an estate called Kilbewley with lodges
and gates and sheep graze over broken walls
the burn bank is all wrinkled like cloth not pulled tight.
I am almost through the shortcut.

But in the last long curve of the road,
birch regrowth on plantation mounds,
nettles and dog mercury, this corner
always slows me down
the sweep of it, the earthworks that hide beneath
the obvious history –

the fact that we curled and grew here together like leaves
and never went back.

Song from the edge

a soft drone from the caravan's generator
your home and a mumble of radio
you were always classy
but drowned by the squeak of holly on glass
and as the wind navigates the factory walls
a chime of hogweed stalks

you live in the mill now
you don't have too
lugging up the shopping
but you prefer its quiet race
the old wheel clogged in its channel
looking back through your tinted window

I see you mouthing the words of a song
something lost and forgotten
if I could I would be here
with my foot on the treadle
waiting for the Friday night dancehall
my pockets as full as your promise

French trees by the roundabout

the wind is like the sound of a supermarket
in a small town where the planted
hornbeams are kicked and scuffed
and gulls far from the harbour

cry at cars just passing lit with the last sun
and a field of cabbages
smelling out hoardings advertising
somewhere else

no plastic bags on
the figure disappearing through the televisions
reflected vehicles yielding amiably
headlights all blown like water

those trees that are always somewhere else
that's the wind tonight
a very slight pollarded suggestion
of a fertile place to end

Glass eels

By the time the European eel (Anguilla anguilla) reach our shores, they have developed into tiny glass eels that swim against the current into Europe's rivers.
—Eels: A Natural and Unnatural History *Christopher Moriarty*

Once elvers, rammed tight like matchsticks,
reflecting burnbridge amid infinite journey
swam a freshwater daytrip in my growing mind:
harvest of eels, jellied fish, or cold alien
yet also translucent and touchable;
they made the water apparent, walkable.

A stream contoured by pencils that map Atlantic
crossing distances science thought too far.
Until tagged eels, one metre muscle, Galway-released,
relocate south using a pump of current
rewriting the subtropical gyre system;
jetpacking open ocean into Caribbean spawnbeds.

At night these eels pulse shallow in warm water:
pilgrims-in-a-desert, they forget food
and spend their days at depth, perhaps
to confuse predators. Contrary coldbath delays spurts,
avoids the lumps and bumps of fertility;
let's them swim sleek by night in streamline.

Until they themselves birth tides.
Eggs hatched into leptocephalus, transparent larvae
in gulfsoup, floating a Sargasso sea furrow;
still shards, the sinuous snap in our tight channels.
And somehow synapse logic breaks.
Somehow the glass eels relight the home burn.